MW01488745

New to Medicare?? Turning 65??

Navigating the Medicare Maze:

A Simple Guide to Medicare

By Kimberly Sikorski

1.-8L5-7 7 O-5 988 (d i rect)
1-800-79 1-5850x101(toll f ree)
kim@libertvmedicareadvisors.com
www.Iibertvmedicareadvisors.com
"Like" us on Facebook @LibertyMedicare
Advisors

Table of Contents

INTRODUCTION

Welcome to Medicare!! Congrats on reaching this major milestone. While this is a very exciting time, it can also be very confusing. This guide was written to help you understand what Medicare is, what it does and does not do and everything you need to know. We will cover the "Parts" of Medicare, how they work and the costs associated with each, how and when to enroll and more. When you are finished reading this guide, you should have a better concept of how to successfully "Navigate the Medicare Maze".

If you have been in an employer plan or have had coverage through the Affordable Care Act (ACA, Obamacare, etc.), you are most likely familiar with how complex and confusing these plans can be. From sky-high premiums and deductibles, never ending co-pays, to limited choices of providers and dwindling networks, you will likely find the change to Medicare can be quite refreshing.

My name is Kimberly Sikorski and I am the co-founder of Liberty Medicare Advisors. We help clients all over the U.S. understand their Medicare options. The goal of this guide is to take the confusion out of Medicare and make the transition as simple and easy as possible. When you know how Medicare works and what your options are, you can make the best choice based on your needs and your unique situation. If at any time you have questions, please feel free to reach out to us and we will be happy to help. You can reach us at 1-800-791-6850, email kim@libertymedicareadvisors.com or find us on Facebook @ Liberty Medicare Advisors. We look forward to being of assistance!!

Now let's get started!!

MEDICARE 101

Let's begin with the basics. What is Original Medicare?

Medicare is health insurance for:

- people 65 and older

- people under 65 with certain disabilities, and

-people of ANY age with ESRD or End Stage Renal Disease (kidney failure requiring dialysis or transplant)

There are 4 basic "parts" to Medicare:

Part A-hospital insurance

Part B-medical insurance

Part C-combines A & B to deliver Medicare Advantage

Part D-Medicare prescription drug coverage

Part A

Think of Medicare Part A as your "hospital" insurance. Medicare Part A covers the following:

-Inpatient Hospital room and board

-Skilled nursing facility care

-Hospice care

-LIMITED home health care

Part B

Think of Medicare Part B as your "medical" insurance. Part B covers the following:

-Doctor's visits

-Services from other health care providers

-Outpatient care

-Part B drugs-includes drugs administered in an outpatient setting such as chemotherapy or other infusions like Remicade

-SOME home health care

-Durable Medical Equipment

-Preventative services

The list of preventative services is rather extensive and includes, but is not limited, to the following:

-Annual Wellness visit

-Breast cancer screenings

-Prostate cancer screenings

-Cardiovascular screenings

-Colorectal cancer screenings

-Flu shots

Many other preventative services are covered. You can find out more in the CMS publication "Your Guide to Medicare's Preventative Services". You can access a copy of this guide on our website under the resources tab. Or you can call or email us and we will be happy to provide you with a copy.

WHAT DOES MEDICARE NOT COVER??

-DENTAL

-VISION

-HEARING

-NURSING HOME/LONG TERM CARE

-FINAL EXPENSES

Medicare Part C (optional)

Medicare Part C is also known as Medicare Advantage. Medicare Advantage plans combine your Medicare Part A and Part B services and usually include Part D prescription drug benefits. Some plans include additional benefits such as some dental and vision benefits. These plans are offered by private insurers. When you sign up for a Medicare Advantage plan, you agree to receive your Part A and Part B services (and usually Part D) through the Medicare Advantage Plan. You are still in the Medicare program. You still have protected rights as provided by Medicare.

Medicare Advantage plans vary widely, but the main thing to keep in mind is that they are typically either an HMO or a PPO, which may limit your choices versus Original Medicare with a Medicare supplement plan. You will also want to look at your plan every year as networks, providers and benefits can change on an annual basis. More on Medicare Advantage coming up soon!!

Medicare Part D (optional)

Medicare Part D is Medicare prescription drug coverage. This is a federal program designed to help Medicare beneficiaries pay for their self-administered prescription drugs. You pay a monthly premium for your Part D plan. The plan may have a deductible and co-pays for the drugs you receive. There are 4 stages involved with Part D plans and we will cover those shortly.

Most plans have a deductible. Drugs are listed in a formulary, which is a list of covered drugs. Each company will have its own formulary and different plans within the same company may have different formularies. Drugs are placed into "tiers" or categories. The tier placement determines the cost for the drug. Lower tiers like tier one and two carry lower copays than say a tier 4 or 5 drug.

Drug plans must offer every therapeutic category of drug, but may not offer a particular drug on their formulary. You can request the drug plan make an "exception" to allow your particular drug if not listed on the formulary. If a drug you require is on a higher tier, you may be able to request the that the drug be allowed on a lower tier. Drug companies may also place "quantity limits" on certain drugs or may require "prior authorization" for certain drugs.

Drug companies have procedures in place to request exceptions to these rules when it will benefit the drug plan beneficiary.

Part D plans vary widely form company to company and even within the same company. Insurance company A may offer 3 different Part D plans, all with differing premiums and different ways the drugs in each plan are covered. It is important to carefully look at Part D options to make sure you are getting the correct coverage as the plans can vary tremendously. You will also need to look at your plan every year as the plans can change on annual basis like Medicare Advantage plans. Having a trusted broker that can do this for can save you time, money and headaches!!

WHAT DOES ALL OF THIS COST??

Now we will talk about what each of these "Parts" cost. Each have a unique set of costs including monthly premiums, deductibles, co-pays and co-insurance.

PART A

For most people, there is no monthly premium for Medicare Part A. This is where all of the Medicare taxes that you or your spouse paid during your working years come into play. If you or your spouse paid Medicare taxes for at least 10 years or 40 quarters, you will most likely receive Medicare Part A without being required to pay a monthly premium.

If you do not qualify for premium free Part A, you may be eligible to purchase Part A. The amount will vary, with the current monthly maximum premium being $458.00. If you paid Medicare taxes for less than 30 quarters, you will pay $458.00 monthly. If you worked for 30-39 quarters, you will pay $252.00

monthly. If you worked 40 quarters and beyond, you will receive Medicare Part A premium free.

Part A Deductibles and co-insurance

The 2020 Medicare part A deductible is $1408.00 per benefit period. It is possible to pay more than one Part a deductible amount in the same calendar year. A benefit period is designated as the first day you are admitted to the hospital or skilled nursing facility and ends when you have been out of the inpatient hospital or skilled nursing facility for 60 consecutive days in a row. If you are admitted again after the 60th day, you will have a new $1408.00 deductible and a new benefit period under which care is received.

You will also have co-insurance amounts due with each benefit period. The co-insurance amounts are as follows:

DAYS 1-60

$0 COINSURANCE FOR EACH BENEFIT PERIOD

DAYS 61-90

$352.00 COINSURANCE PER DAY OF EACH BENEFIT PERIOD

DAYS 91 AND BEYOND

$704.00 COINSURANCE PER EACH "LIFETIME RESERVE DAY" AFTER DAY 90 FOR EACH BENEFIT PERIOD (UP TO 60 DAYS OVER YOUR LIFETIME)

BEYOND LIFETIME RESERVE DAYS

ALL COSTS

Individuals that purchase a separate Medigap plan or Medicare supplement plan greatly limit their exposure to all of the above costs as the Medicare supplement is designed to cover these costs, depending on which plan an individual chooses to purchase. Medicare Advantage plans are also designed to limit the cost associated with a hospitalization, though with most plans you will pay some type of copay for the first several days of being admitted to a hospital. These copays vary widely from plan to plan and will be discussed in more detail in a later chapter.

PART B

Medicare Part B, as mentioned earlier, functions as your "medical" insurance. Think coverage for doctor visits, outpatient procedures and also preventative services, to name a few. Along with a monthly premium, Medicare Part B also has an annual deductible. The Part B deductible for 2020 is $198.00 annually. After you meet your Part B deductible, Medicare will pay 80% of your Medicare approved Part B expenses and you will pay 20% of those costs. Please note that there is no cap on the 20% of costs that Medicare does not cover. Preventative services are typically covered at 100%, not subject to the Part B deductible. Again, there is no cap on the 20% of Part B charges that Medicare does not cover and you are responsible for paying those charges.

Many people choose to add a Medicare supplement plan to help cover what costs Medicare does not pay. More on that in the next chapter.

The standard Medicare Part B premium for 2020 is $144.60. If you earn a higher income, you will be assessed a higher Part B premium (see chart on the next page) If you are receiving Social Security benefits, your monthly Part B premium will be deducted monthly from your Social Security benefit. If you have delayed taking your Social Security benefits, you will receive a quarterly bill. If you prefer to pay your Part B premium on a monthly basis, the easiest way to do this is to set up "Easy

Pay" through Social Security to pay your premium monthly instead of quarterly.

Social Security determines what an individual will pay for Part B premiums. This is based on your MAGI, or Modified Adjusted Gross Income. If Social Security determines you owe a higher premium, you will be assessed with what is known as IRMAA. IRMAA stands for Income Related Monthly Adjustment Amount. If you are receiving Social Security benefits, it will be deducted from your Social Security deposit. If you have delayed benefits, you will be sent a bill by Social Security.

In many cases, you may be able to appeal a Part B premium adjustment. The most common reason to appeal a Part B premium increase is simple. When you retire, your income tends to be lower as you work fewer hours or shift completely out of the work force. Other reasons may include divorce or a loss or reduction in pension. Bottom line, it may make sense to appeal a Part B determination if you can confidently show a change in income. The procedure to file is free and relatively simple. For more information on filing a Part B appeal, see the "Resources" page near the end of this guide.

Medicare Part B 2020 premiums

Individual taxable income	Joint taxable income	Monthly premium
$87,000 or less	$174,000 or less	$144.60
$87,000 to $109,000	$174,000 to $218,000	$202.40
$109,000 to $136,000	$218,000 to $272,000	$289.20
$136,000 to $163,000	$272,000 to $326,000	$376.00
$163,000 to $500,000	$326,000 to $750,000	$462.70
$500,000 or above	$750,000 and above	$491.60

Source: Medicare.gov

PART C MEDICARE ADVANTAGE

Medicare Part C or Medicare Advantage is the optional, alternative way some individuals choose to receive their Medicare Part A and B benefits. When you opt to take a Medicare Advantage plan, you are still responsible for paying for your Part B premium. In addition, you will have the costs associated with your Medicare Advantage plan.

Medicare Advantage plans vary tremendously from state to state, region to region and even county to county. For the sake of discussion, everything in regard to Part C Medicare Advantage is a generalization.

As mentioned above, you will continue to pay your monthly Part B premium. You will then be responsible for paying the premium of the plan that you select. Plan premiums range from $0 monthly to well over $150.00 monthly or more. In many cases, the plans have a $0 or very low monthly premium.

In addition to your monthly plan premium, in most cases, you will pay a copay for most services received under the plan until you reach the plan's annual "Maximum Out of Pocket" amount or "MOOP". The MOOP for 2020 is $6700.00, though some plans may have a lower MOOP. This is the most you can pay for all covered services combined under the plan.

Some copays associated with Medicare Part C plans are office visit copays, ranging from $5.00 to $50.00 or more. Chemotherapy typically carries a 20% charge. You may be charged a daily hospital fee of $150.00 to more than $300.00 a day for the first several days of hospitalization. Copays are also typically assessed on outpatient procedures, diagnostics and more. Keep in mind that while these plans are heavy on copays, they do provide an annual "Maximum Out of Pocket" amount to help limit your exposure.

As you can see, this is just an overview of some of the costs associated with Medicare Part C Medicare Advantage Plans. The actual costs and benefits will vary tremendously from plan to plan and will need to reviewed carefully if you feel this may be the right choice for you.

MEDICARE PART D PRESCRIPTION DRUG PLANS

Medicare Part D prescription drug plans are regulated by Medicare but administered by private insurance companies. Because there are so many plan options and the plans vary tremendously by county, state, region, etc, the monthly premium will vary greatly. Expect premiums anywhere from $15.00 monthly to more than $70.00, depending on the drugs you require. The average seems to be between $15.00 and $25.00 monthly.

In most cases, your plan will have a deductible. The deductible for 2020 is $435.00 annually. Some plans charge a lower deductible amount. Many companies only apply the deductible to drugs in tier 3 or higher. Because plans vary so much, it will depend on the specific plan you choose. It is important to note that it is strongly suggested you sign up for a Medicare Part D when you become eligible EVEN IF YOU ARE NOT TAKING ANY DRUGS. You will avoid a penalty and will have the peace of mind knowing the coverage is in place in the event you need to start taking medication.

Part D plans have 4 stages as follows, each with their own costs:

Deductible Stage-

During the deductible stage, you will typically pay the full amount for your drugs until the deductible is met. The standard deductible is $435.00, but this may vary from plan to plan. Many plans only apply the deductible to drugs in tiers 3,4 and 5. This means you will pay a small copay for drugs in tiers 1 & 2.

Once you reach the deductible amount, you will pay a copay or coinsurance in the "initial coverage stage"

Initial Coverage Stage-

During the initial coverage stage, you will pay your copay or coinsurance (your share of the drug cost) and the plan pays its cost share. The goes on until you reach $4020.00, at which time your enter the "coverage gap" or "donut hole".

Once you reach $4020.00, you enter the "coverage gap" or "donut hole"

Coverage Gap Stage-

It is important to note that most people never reach this stage in their Part D plan. It is important to know what to expect if you should end up in the proverbial "donut hole". During this stage, you receive limited coverage on your drugs. You will typically pay 25% of the cost of your drugs until you reach $6350.00 in out of pocket costs for covered drugs.

Once you have reached $6350.00 in out of pocket costs for your drugs, you enter the final stage of Part D plans which is "catastrophic coverage" stage.

Catastrophic Coverage Stage-

During the catastrophic coverage stage, you will pay a much lower amount for each of your drugs. Typically you will pay 5% for the cost of your drugs or $3.60 for generics and $8.95 for brand name drugs.

Part D drug plans reset every year on January 1st. This means you start all over again with the stages discussed above. Drug plans also can change on annual basis so it is very important to review your coverage annually to make sure your drug plan is the best fit going into a new plan year. A trusted agent or broker should perform an annual review of your drug plan to make sure you are getting what you need.

MEDICARE PARTS A & B
WHEN TO ENROLL

Enrolling in Medicare Part A & B is the next step. It is a fairly simple process and can be completed in a relatively short amount of time. If you are already receiving Social Security benefits, you will be automatically enrolled in Part A and B. You will receive your Red, white and blue Medicare card in the mail about 3 months prior to your 65th birthday.

If you plan to continue working past your 65th birthday and will have creditable employer group coverage, simply return your card to temporarily opt out of Part B coverage. They will send you a new card with Part A only. You will have a "special enrollment period" to sign up for Part B without a penalty when you decide to stop working or you terminate your employer coverage.

If you are not automatically enrolled in Medicare, you will need to enroll yourself, typically during your Initial Enrollment Period. This period is a 7 month window as outlined below.

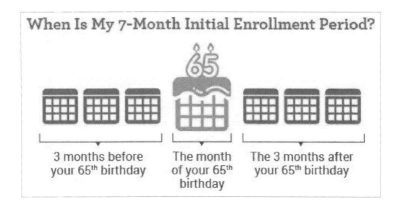

When Is My 7-Month Initial Enrollment Period?

| 3 months before your 65th birthday | The month of your 65th birthday | The 3 months after your 65th birthday |

You can enroll by making an appointment at your local Social Security office, over the phone

(1-800-772-1213) or by going online a www.ssa.gov. We also have the link to enroll conveniently located on our website under the "resources" tab. Visit www.libertymedicareadvisors.com for more information.

Enrolling During a Special Enrollment Period

If you have delayed your Part B because you or your spouse have creditable coverage through employer group plan, you will be granted a Special

Enrollment Period. You will not be assessed a penalty for delaying your enrollment. You can enroll in Part B while you are still covered by your employer plan or during the 8 month window that begins after employment ends or the group coverage ends, whichever is first.

To enroll in Part B during a Special Enrollment Period, there a few easy steps you

will need to take. You will need to have the following forms filled out and sent to Social Security:

-CMS 408(application for enrollment in Medicare)

-CMS L564(request for employment information)

You will fill out CMS Form 408 and your employer will fill out CMS Form L564. When you have the completed forms, it is suggested to hand deliver them to your local Social Security office to be certain they are received. Make sure to make copies of everything. Please note you can request to delay your Part B up to 3 months while you still have employer coverage. Your request will be processed and you will receive a letter from Social Security advising you of their decision.

If you need the forms mentioned above, they can be found on our website under the "resources" tab or feel free to call us(1-800-791-6850) or request the forms via email(kim@libertymedicareadvisors.com) We are happy to help you in any way we can.

MEDICARE SUPPLEMENTS

By now, you can see Medicare provides a great foundation for your healthcare. It does, however, have some gaps in coverage that you will most likely want to cover. Enter the Medicare supplement plan or Medigap plans. In a nutshell, Medicare supplement plans are issued by private insurance companies. They are designed to cover costs that Medicare does not cover, such as Part A coinsurance($1408.00 for 2020 per admission) and the 20% of Part B charges that Medicare does not pay. Let's take a closer look at Medicare supplement plans.

Medicare supplement plans are issued by private insurance companies. The plans are lettered A through N. For the purpose of this guide, we will be discussing Plan G and Plan N (with a few words about Plan F). All Medicare supplement plans are standardized. What this means is that all plans offered must offer the exact same benefits. The only difference you will find is cost. And the cost can vary tremendously from one company to another for the exact same plan.

Some important facts about Medicare supplement plans include:

-If your doctor accepts Medicare, they will accept your Medicare supplement plan.

-There are no networks. You can go to any doctor, provider or hospital ANYWHERE in the United States as long as they accept Medicare.

-No referrals are required.

-Your plan is guaranteed renewable as long as you pay your premium.

-Your plan travels with you

As you can see, there are many benefits to a Medicare supplement plan. Let's take a look at the most popular plans and how the work, starting with Plan G.

Plan G-Plan G is simple. You pay your annual Part B deductible ($198.00 for 2020) and after that deductible is met, Plan G pays 100% of your Medicare approved costs. This includes your Part A hospital deductible and the 20% of Part B expenses that Medicare does not cover. Remember that while Medicare pays 80% of your Part B expenses, the remaining 20% is your responsibility and there is not out of pocket cap on that amount. Your Plan G is designed to cover those charges.

To summarize, with Plan G, you pay your $198.00 Part B deductible. After that is met, your Plan G supplement covers the rest of your Medicare approved expenses.

Plan N-Plan N is another great option that has been gaining popularity as of recent years. Plan N is similar to Plan G in that you are responsible for paying your Part B deductible. In exchange for a lower monthly premium, you may also pay a copay OF UP TO $20.00 for doctor's visits and UP TO A $50.00 copay for an emergency room visit that does not result in an admission. The UP TO $50.00 copay DOES NOT APPY to Urgent Care visits.

Please note you will not pay a copay while you are meeting your Part B deductible. Also note that the copays above are UP TO $20.00. Some visits may be $0 copay or just a few dollars. I also suggest that you plan for the $20.00, though in many cases it will be less.

The other trade-off for a lower monthly premium is that Plan N does not cover the Part B Excess Charges. Typically, this is not an issue and most people will never be exposed to Part B Excess Charges. So what are Part B Excess Charges? Part B Excess Charges occur when a chosen provider does not accept "Medicare assignment". A provider that does not accept "Medicare assignment" can charge the patient 15% over the Medicare rate. With Plan N, you would be responsible for those Excess Charges. However, this is extremely uncommon as approximately 95% of all providers in the U.S. accept Medicare assignment. The easiest way to avoid Excess Charges is to simply ask the doctor if they accept Medicare assignment.

So as you can see, Plan N offers great benefits and typically with a monthly premium 20-30% less than Plan G.

A few words about Plan F-

Plan F has long been considered the "Cadillac" of Medicare plans. It has been the most comprehensive plan as it covers everything Plan G and Plan N cover, but it additionally pays the Part B deductible. In many years past, this had been a pretty good deal. However, the tables have shifted and Plan F has seen premiums rise much more dramatically than other plan letters.

The rules regarding Plan F have changed as well. Due to MACRA, as of January 1st, 2020, you can no longer purchase Plan F if you become eligible for Medicare on January 1st2020 or later. This rule requires all new Medicare beneficiaries to purchase a plan with deductible such as Plan G or Plan N.

Please note that individuals that have Plan F can keep their Plan F. They do not need to do anything. However, they may want to consider switching to Plan G or Plan N if they are able to pass underwriting as Plan F premiums will most likely continue to rise. Individuals that were eligible for Medicare prior to January 1st, 2020 , may also still purchase Plan F, though they will most likely find the premiums for Plan G and Plan N more attractive and affordable. If you have questions about this, please feel free to reach out to our office for more information.

Check out the Medicare supplement chart on the next page.

Benefit Chart of Medicare Supplement Plans Sold on or after January 1, 2020

This chart shows the benefits included in each of the standard Medicare supplement plans. Every company must make Plan A available. Some plans may not be available. Only applicants **first** eligible for Medicare before 2020 may purchase Plans C, F and High Deductible F.

Note: A ✔ means 100% of the benefit is paid.

Benefits	Plans Available to All Applicants (High Deductible G not available prior to July 1, 2019 with an Effective Date – January 1, 2020 or later)										Medicare first eligible before 2020 only		
	A	B	C	D	F	G¹	K	L	M	N	C	F	F¹
Medicare Part A coinsurance and hospital coverage (up to an additional 365 days after Medicare benefits are used up)	✔	✔	✔	✔	✔	✔	✔	✔	✔	✔	✔	✔	✔
Medicare Part B coinsurance or Copayment	✔	✔	✔	✔	✔	✔	50%	75%	✔	✔ copays apply³	✔	✔	✔
Blood (first three pints each year)	✔	✔	✔	✔	✔	✔	50%	75%	✔	✔	✔	✔	✔
Part A hospice care coinsurance or copayment	✔	✔	✔	✔	✔	✔	50%	75%	✔	✔	✔	✔	✔
Skilled nursing facility coinsurance			✔	✔	✔	✔	50%	75%	✔	✔	✔	✔	✔
Medicare Part A deductible		✔	✔	✔	✔	✔	50%	75%	50%	✔	✔	✔	✔
Medicare Part B deductible			✔		✔						✔	✔	✔
Medicare Part B excess charges					✔	✔						✔	✔
Foreign travel emergency (up to plan limits)			✔	✔	✔	✔			✔	✔	✔	✔	✔
Out-of-pocket limit in 2020²							$5,880²	$2,940²					

¹Plans F and G also have a high deductible option which require first paying a plan deductible of $2,340 before the plan begins to pay. Once the plan deductible is met, the plan pays 100% of covered services for the rest of the calendar year. High deductible plan G does not cover the Medicare part B deductible. However, high deductible plans F and G count your payment of the Medicare Part B deductible toward meeting the plan deductible.

²Plans K and L pay 100% of covered services for the rest of the calendar year once you meet the out-of-pocket yearly limit.

³Plan N pays 100% of the Part B coinsurance, except for a co-payment of up to $20 for some office visits and up to a $50 co-payment for emergency room visits that do not result in an inpatient admission.

Enrolling in a Medicare supplement plan-

The best time to purchase a Medic are supplement plan is during your Medicare Supplement Open Enrollment Period. This begins the 1st day of the month you are 65 or enrolled in Medicare Part B. During this 6 month window, you can purchase ANY plan from any Medicare supplement company without being subjected to underwriting. You do not need to "medically qualify" for a plan. The insurance companies cannot turn you down for any reason.

Most insurance companies in most states will apply the same rules during the 6 months (some states are 3 months) prior to your Part B effective date. Why is this a good thing? You can choose your plan, pay the 1st months premium and t lock in your rate without concerns of a rate a increase. This basically gives an 18 month rate lock. You also have the peace of mind of knowing you have this important decision locked down. One less thing to worry about!!

About Medicare Advantage Plans-

Medicare Advantage plans are another way to get your Medicare coverage. Medicare Advantage plans are offered by private insurance companies. You receive all of your Part A and Part B services through the Medicare Advantage plan. Most plans also offer prescription drug coverage. If you have a Medicare Advantage plan, you should not buy a Medicare supplement plan as it will not work with an Advantage plans. Medicare advantage plans typically have low plan premiums in exchange for copays associated with the services you receive. In most cases, you will be in either an HMO or a PPO plan design. You will most likely be subject to a network and may require referrals for certain services and to see specialists. Advantage plans may offer additional coverage like some dental and vision. Advantage plans change on an annual basis do they will need to be carefully looked at year to see if your providers are still in network, how your drugs are covered and what your copays and out of pocket costs look like. The companies issue what is known as an Annual Notice of Change or ANOC every fall. Should you choose a Medicare Advantage plan, this should be carefully reviewed t make sure your plan still makes sense for you.

DESIGNING YOUR PLAN-

Now that you know about Medicare supplement and Medicare Advantage plans, it's time to put this all together and choose the plan that works best for you. Below are the 2 main ways to get your Medicare Coverage.

OPTION 1-

ORIGINAL MEDICARE

PART A AND B

ADD A MEDICARE SUPPLEMENT

MEDICARE PART D PRESCRIPTION DRUG PLAN

OPTIONAL COVERAGE SUCH AS DENTAL, VISON AND HEARING AND CANCER PLANS

OPTION 2-

MEDICARE ADVANTAGE PLAN

(COMBINES PART A & B AND USUALLY PART D)

OPTIONAL COVERAGE SUCH AS HOSPITAL INDEMNITY TO COVER COPAYS, CANCER COVERAGE, ETC

For the sake of this guide, we are going to look into detail at Medicare supplements. Medicare Advantage plans have so many variables with copays, etc that is can be hard to get an accurate picture of what each person will pay. To keep it simple, we will look at a Medicare supplement with Plan G vs Plan N and some optional coverages.

Option 1 Example:

PLAN G=$110.00/MONTHLY
PART D=$15.50
DVH = $40.00
15K CANCER PLAN=$35.00
MONTHLY TOTAL=$200.50

Let's look at the same female with Plan N:
Plan N=$84.00
Part D =$15.50
DVH   =$40.00
15K CANCER PLAN=$35.00
MONTHLY TOTAL=$174.50

Let's look at the optional coverage suggested.

DVH-Dental, vision and hearing plans offer coverage for exactly what they say. Why are these important? Medicare does not cover dental, vision and hearing, so you are left to pay those expenses. These types of plans can be a good way to provide this important coverage ata reasonable cost.

Cancer plans-Cancer plans are becoming popular and really important for seniors and for younger people as well. In the case of Medicare, Medicare and your supplement do a great job of covering for surgery, chemotherapy, etc. Where coverage can fall short is paying for cancer comfort drugs, drugs in the donut hole, paying for travel or special services and more. These plans pay a lump of your choice upon diagnosis of cancer. More and more people are surviving cancer. These plans can help offset the financial sting with a cancer diagnosis.

As far as Medicare Advantage plans go, there are so many different plans and ways to offset copays and costs associated with these types of plans. To get an accurate picture if one of these plans are right for you, you should speak with a Medicare insurance professional that can research and compare your options. Please feel free to call our office for a no-obligation consultation. We are happy to answer your questions and present the options available to you.

WHAT TO DO NEXT...

Now that you know the Parts of Medicare, how it works, costs involved and what your options are to get your Medicare, you need to decide on your coverage and enroll in your chosen plans. You can do this by researching all of the options yourself or you can choose to work with an insurance broker that specializes in assisting individuals in choosing their Medicare coverage.

Here at Liberty Medicare Advisors, we help individuals all across the country understand and choose their Medicare options. We represent all of the top carriers and our advice is unbiased. We do not work for the insurance carriers...we work for you. And we provide our services free of charge. What are some of the benefits of working with a trusted Medicare broker?

-Unbiased advice

-Access to all of the top companies

-Part D comparison

-Access to our assistance with your questions. No need to wait on hold for customer service!!

-MOST IMPORTANT ADVANTAGE IS WE PROVIDE AN ANNUAL REVIEW TO MAKE SURE YOU ARE IN THE RIGHT PLAN WITH THE BEST BENEFITS.

We treat our clients with the utmost respect and strive to provide A+ service on an on-going basis. Our goal is to make this process as simple and easy as possible. We help clients over the phone all across the country. And if you want to "see" us or "see" our offices, we can provide a screen share service so you can see our face!! And remember, our services are always free to you. If you would like more information, please feel free to call us at 1-800-791-6850 or email kim@libertymedicareadvisors.com Be sure to like our Facebook page and check us out on YouTube. You can find both under Liberty Medicare Advisors.

CONCLUSION-

We hope you have enjoyed reading this guide as much as we have enjoyed putting it together. You will most likely have questions and we strongly encourage you to find a trusted Medicare broker that can give you guidance. If you would like to speak with us, we are happy to help answer your questions. Feel free to reach out to us...we look forward to "Helping You Navigate the Medicare Maze"!!

ABOUT THE AUTHOR

My name is Kimberly Sikorski and I am the co-founder of Liberty Medicare Advisors. I have been a Medicare broker for several years and I love helping people understand their Medicare options. Medicare can be complex and I love helping people "Navigate the Medicare Maze". I have written this guide in hopes of making Medicare easier to understand.

When I am not taking great care of my clients, I love cooking, gardening and spending time with my husband and our 2 rescue Labradors, Banzai and Simba. These guys also serve as our "office assistants" and are sure to keep us protected daily from the mail man and the UPS driver.

If you need help with your Medicare options or just have general questions, we are happy to help. Make sure to like us on Facebook for Medicare updates and lots of fun stuff. And visit our website for lots of great resources.

Thank you again for reading this guide.

Sincerely,

Kimberly Sikorski

1-815-770-5988(direct)
1-800-791-6850x101(toll free)

kim@libertymedicareadvisors.com
www.libertymedicareadvisors.com
"Like" us on Facebook @ Liberty Medicare Advisors

RESOURCES

This is a list of resources mentioned throughout this guide. You can go on the web and download them or visit our website under the "downloadable resources" tab. You can find our website at www.libertymedicareadvisors.com

- Medicare & You Guide

- Medigap Buyers Guide

- Medicare Preventive Services Guide

- Medicare Prescription Drug Guide

- Social Security Appeal Guide

Feel free to check out website for additional resources and information you may find helpful. And as always, we are here to answer your questions and assist any way we can.

WHERE TO CALL TO GET QUESTIONS ANSWERED

1-800-MEDICARE(1-800-633-4227)

Get general claims information, request documents and make changes to your Medicare information such as address

TTY: 1-877-486-2048

www.medicare.gov

SOCIAL SECURITY

Find out if you are eligible for Part A and/or Part B, get a replacement card, report address changes, apply for Extra Help with prescription drug costs, ask questions about premiums and report a death.

1-800-772-1213

TTY: 1-800-325-0778

www.ssa.gov

DEPARTMENT OF VETERAN'S AFFAIRS

Contact if you are a veteran or have served in the U.S. military and you have questions about VA benefits

1-800-827-1000

TTY: 1-800829-4833

www.va.gov

DEPARTMENT OF DEFENSE

Get information about TRICARE(TFL) and the TRICARE Pharmacy Program
TFL: 1-866-773-0404
TTY: 1-866-773-0405
www.tricare.mil/tricare4u.com
Tricare Pharmacy Program
1-877-363-1303
TTY: 1-877-540-6261
www.tricare.mil/pharmacyexpress-scripts.com/tricare

OFFICE OF PERSONNEL MANAGEMENT

Get information about the Federal Employee Health Benefits(FEHB) Program for current and retired federal employees
Retirees: 1-888-767-6738
TTY: 1-800-878-5707
www.opm.gov/healthcare-insurance

RAILROAD RETIREMENT BOARD (RRB)

If you have benefits from the RRB, call them to change your name, address or other personal information, check eligibility replace your card or report a death
1-877-772-5772
TTY: 1-312-751-4701
www.rrb.gov

Made in United States
Orlando, FL
29 March 2024

45223003R00026